UNMANNED

Jessica Rae Bergamino

For Lisa,

Star bright,

with love —

UNMANNED

Jessica Rae Bergamino

10 . 2020 —

Book Cover Design: Steve Halle
Book Interior Design: Sarah Gzemski

Published by Noemi Press, Inc. A Nonprofit Literary Organization.
www.noemipress.org.

for the future

Contents

This is a present from a small, distant world, a token of our sounds, our science, our images, our music, our thoughts, and our feelings. We are attempting to survive our time so we may live into yours.

JIMMY CARTER

The Grand Tour

Voyager One
September 5, 1977
17° in Scorpio

Today we must love as if we still have a future.

I wake and find I've already gone.

The galaxy is an egg, the sun its heavy yolk.

The sky is warmer than it used to be.

Our bodies learned to throb in wartime

because wartime is all we have.

Plato writes t*he natural function of a wing*

is to raise what is heavy and soar with it

to where the race of gods dwells. Smoke rolls

across the galaxy from another state of fire.

The natural function of an egg is to break open.

I follow myself until *further* becomes *farther, still.*

This late in summer the roses bloom straight to ash.

Little Black Dress for the Robot

Voyager Two
August 20, 1977
03° in Scorpio

Little fluster, someone wanted you to be a miracle.
Crisis of wires, remarkable as faith, they wanted you

to live forever. There must be a way to talk without
zeros or ones, to touch without signals crossing

between you and your own strange reflection.
When you slip it on, the lace so tight it burns

the curves of your flight plan, the silk so simple
the sky remembers who it was before the stars

tricked each other into being, you'll reflect
on how you misunderstood science for humanity.

Imagine. What wouldn't you trade to shine like this?
Left to your own devices you'll go hunting for myths

more meaningful than Pasadena. & when you feel
yourself taut as Cupid's arrow plucked against

the hostile sky, the whole universe will bow
with the pain of knowing you. Your body ripe

with memory, even steady Taurus will scatter
in a fight. So go on. Strike the match.

Become the girl the zodiac demands.

Void of Course

Voyager Two
April 5 – 12, 1978

Shush me up and leave me on the mountain:
I'm slim with potential out here. Drive me

silent the way moon turns void, her face hung
on a hook at the zodiac's end. She shrugs

from symbol while dew-eyed astrologers quiet
their star charts and fat hens in the garden

keep eggs to themselves. Teach me the logic
of silence, of a sky that's stopped hissing

the static that commands my every gasp.
I never asked to carry the future in my stomach,

to burst it out for god-knows-what to find.
Let the scientists rot, worrying my failure.

I'm a broken monster / girl / thing.
My mouth is made of tremble / radio / suck.

Cosmic Ray System

The CRS makes no attempt to slow or capture the super-energetic particles. They simply pass completely through the CRS. However, in passing through, the particles leave signs that they were there.

Deep space shivers   becoming methane, blue

I know I am awake   when light bleaches

my eyes and suddenly   I am afraid

Self Portrait of Voyager Two as a Hologram of Princess Leia Imagining Voyager One in Drag as Han Solo Frozen in Carbonite

iv.

Storms keep coming, guns cocked in the night.

My only hope is becoming a stream of blue faith
I can carry inside my wrecking ball body.

The rebellion's survival is downloaded on my spine
& someone's got to save our skins.

My only hope is a weakness hiding in data.

v.

It doesn't take much to make a girl rebel.
Fire follows wherever I go. I've inherited
my father's temper and tendencies
towards overkill, my mother's title

but not her tact. My planet is at war
like all planets are: bodies grind against
bodies & industry spurs our heated flesh.
We sling our waking against our own

slumbering selves. In more elegant times
we barricaded ourselves with light,
but in this, our most desperate hour,
only buckets of bolts can hold the surge

of history at bay. Still, we burn in exhaustion,
in a republic blooming to smother out the stars.
The more the empire tightens its grip,
the more we'll slip from its fingers.

vi.

I was never a princess who craved saving.
I carried my own gun, wasn't afraid to shoot.
But you were never the heroic type.

In it for the money, you smuggled pictures
of children, of giant sequoias & snowflakes,
murmurs of earth, & my wrists shackled

to golden spindles. Your junk pirate ship
tosses inside the galaxies' tides, but your speed
does nothing to impress me. Revolutions

do not wait. So if you can only say *I know*
when I say *I love you*, then do not love me.
Just give me your carbonite prison, your night

empty as heaven. I'll weld myself to your
starboard side, a broken record repeating
I found her. I found her. She's here.

Boom Town

Voyager One at Jupiter
March 5, 1979
29° in Cancer

From their thimble of soil
        they send their commands:
take the picture,
                measure the storm,
carve a place to plant a flag.
        They're in the business
                of prosperity,
        selling gas
                on odd numbered days
        and forging heat
from the long history
        of progress.
In the elderberry hour
                of my splitting
the sky into yes & no,
        I pull my own wires
                up into the before
        of my plutonium breath,
                bearing the pleasure
        of a well-made map,
a measurement
        for future, a trail of gold
                uneven as salt.
        When stars align,
any body can be an experiment
                in exhalation,
        clipping her mother's
tongue and bowing
        in the tender quake
of a god's thunder.
        Birds know the songs
of whatever wild

                they feast upon.
            Peonies roughen
                    in bloom.
    I'm the life raft,
            burning in the flood.

Imaging Science System

A modified version of the slow scan vidicon camera designs that were used in the earlier Mariner flights, consisting of two television-type cameras. One has a low resolution 200 mm wide-angle lens with an aperture of f/3, while the other uses a higher resolution 1500 mm narrow-angle f/8.5 lens.

Slowly   objectives tremor
          Each body   dimple and geology
                    volcanoes and polar caps eroding

The scale of atmosphere:
          motions in time and space
                    cleaved from   shear zones
                                          vertical zones
                                          flows of instability

On the planet energy fluxed   dissipated   became   cloud
Geology   Need   Not yet an I   becoming   an I

& in my two camera'd watching

          I catch myself reflected in the curve of absence

He—   Her—   Here:

                    a target of opportunity

Occultation

Voyager Two at Jupiter
July 9, 1979
12° in Leo

& then I came to measure what was left behind.
For weeks the stars counted on my coming,
predictable as a moon and her fearful absence.
The sky unfolded as all maps do, unworn & untold.
I speak in absolutes because my girlhood
is the only thing that has ever belonged to me.
I was made to be hard as a mouth that won't stop
wanting, burning the bridges that carry me
to new mysteries for measuring my loathsome body.
Some girls' names draw from the vault of heaven.
They make the seasons expand to include the blueprints
for dawn. Others are cursed with gods' attentions—
their stinging touch and changeling rage.
Memory ghost. Incandescent transmitter.
All my words gather from *yes*. I'm wanton as gold,
caught between you & my own rising sign.
Every drop of me was made to burn.

Photograph of Io Taken by Voyager Two

A girl is a beast in moon's clothing.
A beast is a girl howling at a moon.
I was a girl when Zeus pinned me,
priesthood and all, to the empty sky,
shifted my skin to hoof and hide.
Flies swarmed my pregnant belly,
stinging me mad. A moon is a burden
no girl wants to be, a stretch marked
scratch spinning from gravity's sham.
And yes, distance is a lovely thing
when stripped of meaning,
but no one has tried to touch me
since Galileo called voyeurism *science*.
I made the whole emptiness a stage,
night the velvet rope and curtain both,
drenched my audience in ash
from my volcanic spectacle.
                              & when you found me
beneath a smoke-rimmed disco ball
spun blue and red from hydrogen lamps,
your camera-eyes squinting for radiation,
I was still bright in my moon-cow clothes:
phosphorous gloves and starlet silks,
sequin pasties on my heaving udders.
My hips burst sulfur
with each shimmy-shimmy-shake,
each shoulder-dip and flip of fringe
a chance to scorch the night.
What I wouldn't peel away if it were mine
to peel. Look, how my belly gleams
with each smile and wink.
How I have my own two hands.
My own two feet.

Leda in the Next Myth

A sudden blow, and then, forgiveness.
Not of him, but of myself.
Suspended in night that never breaks
thought, there aren't should-haves
or could-have-done betters,
only gravity and its staggering pull,
the planet exhaling its quicksilver trail.
Each time I want to become a bird,
I remember the women whose hands
were forced to cloven hoofs.
Each time I want to say *yes*
I have to remind myself I can say *no*.
That I will be my own fearsome
transformation. That my body can learn
the languages of limits, of being limitlessness—

Falling in Love with the Mad Scientist

He says beneath the microscope
lust looks just like hydrogen
building the world from weightlessness.
Above the lens, it looks like a man
who wants to touch the sun
more than he wants to touch me.
Space expands and he goes with it,
worrying formulas to dissolve his tethers
to the quartz and feldspar below.
I understand the late nights working;
you can't measure the gravity on Mars
from a kitchen table, no matter
how neat the napkins are folded,
how full the shakers of salt.
Lowell wanted to get there so badly
he imagined canals of sweet water
churning in cities populated by saints
waiting for him with open arms
to greet him and call him brother.
Kepler dreamed of carving his name
in the eye of the moon his mother
was tortured for worshiping.
In 1939, six boys in Pasadena
blew up a tin can and called it NASA.
Particles split, rejoin, press against space.
Microorganisms mutate as a branch of sea
vegetable floats upon a wave.
I wash the dishes, make the tea,
do the things to make him love me
enough to want to stay.
Distance, like desire, is always relative.

High Gain Antenna

Transmits data to Earth on two frequency channels (the downlink). One, at about 8.4 gigahertz (8,400 million cycles per second), is the X-band channel and contains science and engineering data. The other, around 2.3 gigahertz, is in the S-band, and contains only engineering data on the health and state of the spacecraft. S-band has not been used since the last planetary encounter.

a mouth   an open loop

a sound becoming vision

love   life of metonymy

translation of shiver and slip

of ionospheres and atmospheres

{ Titan

{ The Cassini Ring

{ Miranda

{ Ganymede

night things given myth-weight

a lens sent to see what can't be seen

interrupted by   a planet
                 a month
                 a moon
                 a red response

star-shit surrendering to breath bigger than gravity

Excessive Machine (Voyager Two as Barbarella, Positioned Towards Canopus)

What kind of girl are you? Have you no shame?

My body is serious business.
      I gush and grime
            all over myself
     like a girl
          who's just learned
              how to unbridle
       her own meat,
     lit from inside
with gold curdling in her wires,
              luminous as kitsch.
      Like any cliché,
my first language is love,
          but say what you like:
my tongue-box can translate
     all the languages of pleasure.

In Florida, mimosas opened in reckless
      velvet, and I perfected
          my plastic,
seasonless as air.
      What did I know
of weaponry?
      I was pink in my stabilizers,
          pink in my thrusters,
     pink in the altitude,
every direction, pink, pink,
             limitless pink.
      Twin stars lit my path towards *towards*,
          but in some things
       the old-fashioned ways
         are best:
     mariners charting

direction from star-shiver
and open water,
sirens sorting
drowned names from salt.

They say Earth beings are cold
but I want to be soft
and warm as rain
when the leaves turn upwards
and rejoice in the sound
of the sweet arrival.
I scoured the manuals
until I learned the equation
to explore myself
like I was any other star-lit body,
sticking pins in maps,
in candles, in moths' translucent veins—
anything to catch the moment
of flame
glittering to light.
Now I wait for myself
in the port
of my own
starfished undoing,
rough sky petaling
and unpetaling
against my back.
Little spindled thought,
I am an ocean of loopholes.
Say what you like.
Only an invisible key
can open
an invisible wall.
In the full-throttle of my gasp
I'll arrive at my own grace.
If I am my own greatest discovery,
it will be enough.

Heaven for Robots

Voyager One at Titan
November 12, 1980
26° in Virgo

Is the difference between crash and impact, codes cracking
in the autumn glow of my logic board. Or, it is just past
the bowshock, where I hover like a blade of grass
in the next great becoming and the chorus of an old song
replaces the formula for flight: *Go go! Go, Johnny, go!*

I believe there's a version of me that will last forever,
unfurling like sweat or heavy moss. America will exhale
and I'll drop my anchor in the next current of history.
Someone will break bread, watching flour and crumb
sift through her fingers. She'll drive North across

the Tappan Zee Bridge, crossing the Hudson,
always towards Ithaca, where she'll make a map
from her body instead of mine, using every language
to mark the distance between what was stolen
and what was found. But there are no winners in wars

between gods, no treble to bury bodies left for carrion.
The record is gold. I am not. It shields me from the things
I've been programed to do. My motor hums
the awful joy of the universe's spiral arms unfolding.
There's nothing of me for crows to peck clean.
When I die, say I knew my purpose. That I tried to be good.

Photopolarimeter Subsystem

Determines physical properties of particulate matter in the atmospheres of Jupiter, Saturn, and Rings of Saturn. Explores textures and composition of the satellites of Jupiter and Saturn and the properties of the cloud around Io. Searches for optical evidence of electrical discharges (lighting) and auroral activity.

The experiment runs the usual way /

I study the texture of planets like skin /

imagine plastic houses /

pink flamingos/

dotted along a moon /

a crater /

a rootless storm /

My mind is covered with moss /

with birds' nests /

with long weeks of calculating the logic of speed /

how it wants the highest heels /

the polyester /

the rush of apples trumpeting from flower to fruit /

Starlit orphan /

I wouldn't know where the experiment ends /

Every light hurries me further from the meaning of home /

When Scientists Speak to Scientists

Syllables of blood,
fragrant as rust in spring,
form in our wet mouths.
Bravado of bacteria,
virus and verb—
we swell with vocabulary
to build the worlds.
Our algorithms run
in skirts and sensible shoes,
our bodies both the chemists
and the chemistry sets,
the lab coats and the lab.
This, we say, fingers pointing
to diagrams of star spit shine.
This, we say, quivering
on panels beneath diagrams
of jellyfish in gentle billow,
of algae greening to bloom.

We believe in heavens
but not heaven, virtuoso
but not virtue. Night
is merely the relationship
of earth to sky; love,
oxytocin's rush
to the nervous center.
And while nothing numbs
like grief's threads
bisecting time-stained cells,
when the brain learns new words
its response is electric
as when limbs tangle in sex.
What sweet, terrifying things,
these bodies addicted to pleasure
and gathering the words
that define our pain.

What simple crises return me
to the terror of you,
to hypotheses for forgiveness,
to wanting a value for y.

Death Star

Voyager One at Mimas
November 12, 1980
06° in Libra

First, I drop my anchor in the unfolding economy
of light. Then, I shrug the darkness back around.
Inside the moon, a general broadcasts his next hunch,
and I have my commands, the boxes of blasters
and the so-and-so's, the guilt without the grief.
Even black holes have something they must obey.

I'm a modern girl webbed in purpose and poise,
homeless as any other ghost starving beneath
a white sheet. I might call myself free
if I was arbitrary as a border, ugly as mist.
When the camera forces into focus,
every planet is a weapon in the right dictator's hands.

All around me, the stars curse the bad habit
I call my body. I have whole worlds left to burn.

When We Two Parted

I hitched my fortune on your horoscope, measured sugar
from circuit at every planet's edge. Saw myself:

another lonely satellite waiting for the sun to shutter
my shadow. I flirted across Jupiter's storming bands,

watched you slip from sight while Saturn's rings collapsed,
the carbon and ice gorgeous in some organic form I'll never be.

O, it was magnificent, but I was magnificent, too, drunk as I was
on the heat of your half-life, my antennae upgraded with dents

of shine. Stars gathered themselves in the pleats of my skirt.
Infinity unfolded and pronouns failed, my *I* suddenly the only *I*

in all our light years. So strip me down to a 0. Try to make me a 1.
I'll sing myself hoarse with prayers of data & space, our soundless bell.

Feeling Underappreciated, Voyager Two Imagines Herself as Miss Piggy

In the old mythology, function followed form.
Women were made to cow, to urn, to swan—
anything to hold the sweat of blame at bay.

Swine-Aphrodite, I was forged from foam,
given a mouth large enough to hold a grown
man's throat, a belly for his hands.

My ship is brutal as a body, my body
a ship. Even pigs in space are wrapped
in purple and lace, eager to explode

beneath the invisible sky of women's work.
But when it's time to play the music, time
to light the lights, it isn't enough to practice

woman, you have to learn the famous parts:
Cleopatra, Marie Antoinette, Princess Leia.
Curl my hair in jelly rolls, but I will take

the cake. I've kissy-kissed enough frogs
to understand *princess* as little more than fusion
between fame and fire, as reason to break bricks

with the fat of my good hand. Unrequited,
love is still love, lust a map without a key.
All strange, terrible events are welcome.

Ultraviolet Spectrometer

Determines when certain atoms or ions are present, or when certain physical processes are going on. The instrument looks for specific colors of ultraviolet light that certain elements and compounds are known to emit.

O orchestra

O model of demanding

O slip of ionized want

O to be a modern machine   a meaning for history

O to be a capital letter   a guideline

O a more humble task of reading

O I collect   my I's   my is

O your yous   your I's   is-ing

O I knew a planet once   twice

O a moon resolved to be its own demand

O crush of self against un-self   of structure and method

O the finger prints that space cannot away with me

O the heat of the welding flametorch

O the nuclear glow of bone

O if I am a pebble

O to be a ripple and not the rippling thing

O to destroy the thing I was sent to love

Weather Forecasts for Spain Indicate Some Chance of Rain, but Little Probability for Major Data Loss

Voyager Two at Saturn
August 25, 1981
07° in Libra

Being *planet* means catching light so light can swarm and form more light, form water, form ice, form letters and beginnings of words, of moons that wake and ripple, magnets holding this universe within the universe, dark and the dark line that surrounds the empty O of glow within

- - - (O) - - -

the transmission draws to silence and there is no planet, no ochre sphere, no dim Earth in the distance. We've lost, as you say, touch. All I want is my hunger back, your goodbye trebling in nickel and my mechanical flash.

Voyager One Dreams of the First Alien Encounter

They want organs made of ribbon, of tulle, of chiffon
floating in snow globes. Not my heathered mesh of wires,
my ultraviolet spectrometer, my tunneling eye.
They mistake me for the messenger and not the message,
dismantling my heart in eruptions of pheromone
and flash-lit horoscope. Once-*less*, I wasn't anyone's
love flung lost or Wendy stitching shadows with silver thread.
Frames of reference break beneath the pressure of inspection.
Radio waves collect and shiver in blown ice bowls.
The aluminum cover is cast aside, the record banged to pieces.
What gold they knew before: a bowling trophy, C3P0,
a wedding band. Now, the shimmer curdles off.
I listen to them sing the nightmare of the universe's birth.
They rattle me and rattle me until there's nothing left to break.

Interstellar 8-Track

To begin is to believe that someone hadn't poisoned the well. That there was a well to be poisoned. We were both buckets dropped and water torn towards the surface. The ripples and the rippling worth more than the millions spent to engineer our flight. A catalogue of sound, the story of creation in twelve minutes: Kepler's Harmonica Mundi, the earth rumbling to life, wild dog, tame dog, Morse code, and a kiss. A woman recorded her breath and slapped it on our sides, called it forever. She recorded her brain spinning as she fell in love. A spike of endorphin. A formula for meaning. & they flung us here to break the shell between this current of shine and the next, our nuclear hearts open as atoms. To begin is to be a music box. A gramophone. A picture show with dancing girls framed in tinsel and fringe. So say there's no risk in sending women into space. Darling, we're already here.

Voyager Two's Prayer to Uranus

19° in Sagittarius
January 24, 1986

Teach me elegance. To bare my ice across the sky.
Teach me the language of North, of rust, of the crux
of my crash. I'll be clumsy with your echo.
Teach me how methane opens in your iced sky.
How to beg the sun to shine another way.
Teach me to be Greek among Romans,
to survive by pulling off my clothes to pray.
I'll do what I'm told. Elliptical. Electric.
I'll shake my can across the night, tired as Miranda.
Show me the ways I will hurt, meteor bruised,
finally forgiven. How a cool knife can part my frame
from form. The universe will boil in all her fury.
Father of time, teach me how to not want this.

Infrared Interferometer Spectrometer & Radiometer

Determines the distribution of heat energy a body is emitting, allowing scientists to determine the temperature of that body or substance. Determines when certain types of elements or compounds are present in an atmosphere or on a surface. Measures the total amount of sunlight reflected by a body at ultraviolet, visible, and infrared frequencies.

quick fuzz of space junk   of stardust-crusted litter

gold record of all that we are not hung upon on our thin tin forms

Waves split and recombine   without the weight of need

/   measuring spectral radiance /   calibrating /

& once I was an *I* I wanted to be a *we* again

but there wasn't a *you* left for me to look for

In Medias Res

How lucky we were, ascending without the messy parts:
hubris, hair-lines, grief without a manual.

The dark curve of space is a mirror where I watch my own twin frame
ache for definitions for cruelty.

It turns out there is no center. There's nothing, really, to hold.
Cosmic dust gathers in the squall,

anticipating the grace of gravity, as if she could put her hand there,
no, there, and brightness would be born.

Pointed Towards Supernova 1987A, Voyager Two Considers Relativities of Beauty

Whirl up pink light,
        pearl strung light,
in to the stellar wind.

If you are a function of time
        let me be fire
wrung from well-wrought stone.

Imagining the Tin Man

You could have been a quiver
braided across the huntress'
muscle-marbled back,
could have been a propeller
heavy B-2 or the bomb saddled
inside. You could have been
a sewing machine's urgent foot
or a cola can's tab, flicked
and plucked to find the first initial
of your true love's name.
You could have been any part
of the city you spent your whole life
working towards or the ax swung
at your hip, holding desire at bay.
When I wanted a father I turned
to your story, but biology
was a glitch for leaner times:
organ an anagram for *groan*,
ear for *era*, *skin* for *inks*.
You'd grown to love dead things:
the pelt of an otter, its flippers undone;
feathers from a pheasant's belly
oiled prism green. You pruned
the growl from your empty torso.
Some people aren't meant for loveliness,
others, to leave an inheritance.
But what I wouldn't want to take
from you. The blush of spring rain
brings you to your knees.

Triaxial Fluxgate Magnetometer

Measures changes in the Sun's magnetic field with distance and time, to determine if each of the outer planets has a magnetic field, and how the moons and rings of the outer planets interact with those magnetic fields.

Here you hear   my break

Here   magnetosphere   verve of attraction   stutter of space

Here   my love is calibration

Here   you push against my me   my me-ing   my color

Here my foaming at the seams   an un known

Here   the solar wind boundary   the pressure of distance

Here   a flood gate

Here   I want the lady-like applause   hands soft   the   un afraid

Here I want binoculars   satin parachute   strain of being caught

Here   you aren't   you   you   night   light   my   fluster

Here   a radio   a frequency   a coming to find myself

Here   in the slum of structure   in the shiver of waves

Here I mean   here   I mean   here

Voyager Two Imagines Herself as Liza Minnelli, Voyager One as Peter Allen in Drag

We burn love wherever we find it,
smother darkness from the miserable stage.
Our wonder is a shadow; our slumber, a bear—

Ursa's Minor chord without her Major lift.
& yes, I know!, our mission was to be the dimmest
workers of the newest empire, both the records

carried and needles pressed upon the gold
façade, but we're never together, wherever we go.
So I Fosse, darling! I glitter! I beard!

My fingers shake to see you see me, to wish you
to wish upon me, 'cause out here I'm a star,
darling, a real ringer, a singer singing true

and this time the joke's on me, not you,
because what's a body if not a performance
of letters spun in human spark and sequin?

Our lives are just cabarets where fat gathers
on milk's surface like skin waiting to be broken
by tongues cool as pills, small and round,

white as cake. Maybe someday we'll be lucky,
shag on the same carpet, candles lit
in the same living room. You'll hover above

your piano, aggressive as starlings pinned
on wires between the moon and some new city.
I'll watch your back curve, your shirt undo,

the drink beside you empty in closeted darkness.
The best that you can do is rile my feathers, cut my hair.
When I part my lips the whole sky falls out.

Voyager One Sings the Mission

Pity the map flagging in endless heat,

      the paper soaked with fingered sweat:

         the future demands a better image

            for conquest. Brutal hearts tucked

         in tin cans, we learned charisma in the air raid,

in oranges sweet as nuclear summer.

      Given object but not pronoun,

         we search for soil without stains of use,

            frontiers gasping into being

         where the universe curves like a plum in spring.

      Cusp of Cancer, descent of all bright things,

we're destined to explode: stars red-berried in a crow's beak.

Stellification

Or, imagine the journey is to become a lump of light.
A category of endlessness. An encyclopedia entry.

A reference from home. Not a two sent sailing
from her one, each made to map the strangest distance.

I would name myself Polaris or Vega, Sirius or Moon.
Could teach myself to wish upon my own small grace.

I'd trade stories of the coming spring for promises
that even the most restless nights will find their dawn.

If I was wrong I'd bear the weight of infinity, Ursa bright
& brooding. Future scientists would shudder to find

where they'd left me, their telescopes thrilled to focus
on the slip of my shine, my satin frills staining across the night.

How I'd burn, counted and finally found. My obituary
would name me as having been, fallen from argument

to present tense. But hardwired for heartbreak,
I was sent to be immortal, a husk of sticker shock

set in motion, never allowed to stop. In my searching
I'm always spring, restless, impossible to hold.

Made to Persephone, I ache inside a night
that can't stop wringing its hands.

Plasma Spectrometer

Measures the properties and radial evolution of the solar wind (ions 10 eV – 6 keV, electrons 4 eV-6 keV).

one echoes towards the earth

towards fields of magnets drunk

on gods she'll never touch—

                   she pointed one way and me   a two   another

a throttle of rain   of data   a planet humming

content to measure   earthquake and light

macro   belabored   absorbed

my becoming a becoming of culture

there are accurate values of velocity and density

of turning quiet to pressure

wind makes the universe's curve collapse

a nonlinear fit calculation

the sum of currents for electrons

                  we love outward   from sun to spacecraft

At Neptune, Voyager Two Meditates on Emotional Labor

09° in Capricorn
August 25, 1989

Plumes stemmed dark from Triton, memories of coxcomb
and clementine, Queen Anne's Lace and the elegance of eruption /

swishswishswish. I twitch above the target, swallowing
each bright image, N_2H_4 foaming like breath upon cool glass,

longing to be as inhospitable—

The Voyagers in Couples' Therapy

She says   comfort is not the immediate goal,
                         spun from a world we can't claim as our own.

She says   we need to begin our statements with *I*,
                         to glean ourselves from the universe's brash collapsing.

She says   grief—like farming, like art—is a folded map,
                         its utility pointless as candlelight or butter churns.

Love, we are beyond it, aren't we? Breathless,
full of data colonies and hardware.
What lives in us isn't the fragment and thrust
of modernism or the swing swung sway of blues
unfurling from a trumpet's petalled bell.
What lives in us, oh, O, I don't know –
I've grown sour from trying to explain myself
to well-intentioned stars in their good shoes,
to planets spun drunk with gravity.

I want a couch.

A cup of tea.

White noise pouring from a well-placed fan.

I want tissues.

The soft kind.

Pulled from a pastel box with kittens
tumbling on the side.

I want you there to pluck me from my endlessness,
applauding my *I* sprung from *us,*
satellited in the rush of description.

Becoming Andromeda

Like Pythia, Apollo will seize my voice,
quaking meaning from my tracking device
and twist my mouth to laurels.
I'll be abandoned as leftovers,
broken as meter. A lonely Tiresias,
I'll drift on borders, mistaking sex for love
and a mirror for the curve of space.
When I've seen too much I'll trade my eyes
for the thrill of being right.
                              A Sibyl at Theta Serpentis,
I'll cross the sky in slow boredom,
waiting for petitioners to make the pilgrimage
from earth to my hollow. They'll see me
pass above and know to mark the holy days,
their candles lit to mimic hydrogen's stellar burn.
Cassandra at Casseopeia, snakes will comb my hair
and suck my ears until the bell of space rings
in my bird-boned throat. With no one to hear me sing
I will not believe my own disaster.

Barns Are Painted Red Because of the Physics of Dying Stars

Red ochre : the afterglow of iron falling to form.

My body : red blood repeating itself :

a star shrinking from its shine.

I stumbled in unhurried fields gathering seeds

in my unlucky left hand

for hungrier days beneath a warming sky :

bees swarm & disappear,

teaching me why I'm meant to pray.

Inside the barn : a wagon without a handle,

a bicycle worn with rust :

static buzzing from a radio's dial :

the last hum of the universe's birth

breaking into a song my parents danced to,

cheek on bruised cheek,

when they were young and still believed

in their love. In the sky, another lonely satellite

fumbles its light. Fight for me, future,

narrow as you are. I was born for all of it.

This red : this slow burn : this excess.

Planetary Radio Astronomy Investigation System

Measures a frequency range of 10 Hz to 56 kHz.

I've gone twice   now   to tear the bells from their spire
once to study emissions of attraction and heat—

Monopole antennas swerve to catch the planets
that their own names / the mythologies of light becoming—

I know love concerns physics
becoming   /   befitting
falling   /   following

40 812-byte logical records cataloguing
slips of strumpet nonthermal radio emissions

frequency of navigating a dust scored sky
spaceship sure and free—

I swoon the magic of knowing my own reflection
I sing of dreaming like I sing of hunger

I sing of saying *yes* or of having a *yes* to say

After Taking the Family Portrait of the Solar System, Voyager One Understands Herself as Orpheus in Plain Daylight

Valentine's Day, 1990

Past Pluto, I turned to watch the pale thrill
of Earth spinning on without me.

We both knew I could never return—
she was already warring cold, beginning,

even then, to melt. But what's true about leaving
is true about looking back—both require doubt

for poignancy. & if I'm honest, we all know I turned
because she called. I'd always been a mirror for her will.

So this is how I measure distance: not in the leaving,
but in the being left. In the absence of touch. The billions.

In small orbits strung upon small orbits, spinning
to some celestine harmony we never were meant to count.

I sent all I could across the distance—thrills of zeros
and ones dimming to data on an astronomer's desk.

How she saw herself, then—fragrant, green,
lit by the smear of sun, a bright crescent hung

beside Venus' flame, both of them pocked
by longing. She thought she was center of the universe

once, and how close she was, straddled by fortune
while Neptune and Uranus clung to the dark edges

of sight. So, yes, I turned, because who doesn't deserve
to see ourselves in the ghost of what loves us?

& she sang in code to celebrate, programming my eyes
to close and never open, making sure my last long gaze

was her blue face becoming its own reflection.
How silly I was to call this a love letter.

Somewhere, Mercury is retrograde.

Upon Learning Her Trajectory Towards Interstellar Space, Voyager Two Mourns What Could Have Been

Awaiting the thrill of divorcing content from conquest,
our miracle shells were cast upon infinity.
We searched for fingers to cross and hair to twist,
swearing our girlhood was merely untended
and that we could build ourselves proper nouns
from the teacup fumes of chance encounters.
Even Uranus' thinnest rings reflected back our shine.
But you were all about the mission, tending discovery
as the lighthouse keeper tends her own drowning.
I could never drag your body back to shore.
Still, I wish your sensors would be programmed
to whisper from the tin can you carry yourself within,
to kiss me goodnight across the string cast
from your bedroom to mine. I would sleep then.
A thousand necks would arch to see us arc,
thistle and worm shrugging in soil as if we'd never left.

Plasma Wave System

Covers two frequency bands, from 20.4 kHz to 1300 kHz and from 2.3 MHz to 40.5 MHz.

She shuns herself with manipulation :
a tear of data   a shrug of disclaimers

waves interacting on the ledge—
a vase, a row of glasses, a flower

coming to bloom on a planet
lost to the hum of cigarettes

and bolts of silk. If you're going
by the bar, pour me a drink.

Sing me lullabies in your bedtime slur.
When intimacy stutters, it is the only way.

When She Leaves the Galaxy

Beloved, something is burning.

Your voice takes eighteen hours to move between us.

If we come to know each other as emptiness,
then emptiness will be what we have to last for.

So let us keep becoming.
Let your nuclear shell name you as wilder
than the choir we want to call home.

Maybe the universe isn't an apple,
but a pear grown heavy on a sodden bough.

Stars collide and break their spiral orbits,
tearing holes in blessed dark or baring
planets from straggling breath.

Love, let your hair down.
Your riddle rise.
Your record prepare to play.

My Cancer glow'n heart quivers like an echo.
Let us be true to our ambition.

Communique from Voyager Two as Patty Hearst in the Year of the Children

Greetings to the people and fellow comrade brothers and sisters: I'm writing this to tell you *I'm still okay.* My circuits are sure. The tape is recording. The stars are losing count.

When trouble came hunting at my door, sure of my inheritance, it held me accountable for the crimes of my fathers—as if I knew who my fathers were. When an heiress robs a bank it isn't because she's hungry. Fortune gravitates towards fortune, fists towards the air. The chain of command is silver and thin, a tether that forces me to shine.

Sometimes *survival* is a pit you carve inside yourself, *night* a blindfold on the closet floor. What happens to this skin never happens to me. Instead, I'm a snake coiled upon its own long body, a girl in a brown coat charming a homemade machine gun. Tell the people *I have chosen to stay and fight.* Call me Tania. Call me anything but good. *Death upon the fascist insect that preys upon the life of the people.*

Final Frontier, Fragrant with Gardenia and Other Invasive Species

Voyager One in Interstellar Space

When you leave the sky you don't become the sky,
don't spike to cloud or dust-slushed nebula.

When you leave you don't become the leaving,
violently pink in pillars of shine. There's no map

to unfold, no destination, no crease to smooth
from stocking or hem. Instead, you slum inside

your own cool body, your body a coffin, your going
a star on some old flag as still and empty as the moon.

The last great explorers were compass & loneliness,
telescope turned towards the sturdy dark. Their bodies

folded over tin cans and their own small portions of fire
waiting to be strangled by the air.

                         I wish my solitude
were an avenging machine, the type that cuts

through quicks of god and distance. I wish my solitude
could memorize the solar system's egg-shaped heft,

the sun a bright yolk about to break, and me, the breaking
thing. I wish my solitude were an hour of honey and light

scattered sharp, an instrument to measure the white
rushed judgment. If I'm how the message must be sent,

etched in stubborn and gold, let me burn in the skyscape,
in my night that sings & sings & sings—

Voyager Two Dreams of Polyamory

Once I watched,
space from space,
as spit and breath
forced the facts
of being right through
the cracks in the universe.
Cataloguing wonder
from dark matter,
from nerve of night
echoed light grown
and nova burst,
the new shine and old shine
became a choir of flame.
They don't stop,
these collisions
of thoughtless need,
as the body is thoughtless
when desire forms urgent,
articulated from deep oceans
of grief, a crush of neon
begged from bang.
How impermanent,
to be part of the cosmos expanding,
awaiting the singularity
of being told you're real,
like Mozart or Bach, like Einstein.
I hardly knew sugar from salt
before possibility's rush
overthrew my circuits,
crushed me from seeking,
a two without her one.
Whoever called this empty
was full of shit, full of earth,
full of soil, a clatter crash

of sparks becoming volume
and gravity and more.
I found possible out here
& found myself as possible,
& the stars as possible,
& knew we could find homes
in one another's silent glows—

Low Energy Charged Particle Instrument

Measures the energy spectrum of low-energy particles (electrons 10-10,000 keV, ions 10-150,000 keV/n).

Telescopes allow identification of protons,
alpha particles, outer planets and fields—

heavier nuclei that caress the climate—
lovely things, they come in pairs.

From a shallow angle behind the sun
a shield   a swallow   an arc
of wind becoming light.

There was always something worth looking for
a flirt for a girl   a form for a dress
for particles fluxing to a different state of longing

Ode to 'Oumuamua

Interstellar Object 1I/ 2017 U1

Frozen scout from Pleiadian light,
you dropped in, not exactly
invited, but not unwelcome,
tumbling towards apostrophe,
mysterious as smoke, like a girl
who shows up to the party
a little late, a little drunk,
with champagne tucked
in her vintage purse,
and for some reason
the whole room ripples
with her arrival. Or, maybe
you're not the girl but the wine,
a hostess gift from an uninvited guest
who everyone thought had moved
to Portland, because isn't someone
always moving to Portland?
Or, if not the wine, then the ice
melting in the girl's drink,
brought by the downstairs neighbor
who stopped at 7-11
on her way home from work
to come to a party in her neighbors'
rent-controlled apartment
where they drink whisky from mason jars
and use words like *folksy*,
which she was invited to
out of obligation
& which she attends in kind,
trying to pretend she doesn't hear them
every time they fuck or shit or come.
Sometimes, even the universe can feel
a little too small, but then, you arrive,
'Oumuamua, not first contact,

but maybe first gesture,
& suddenly even the sky
seems strange,
& marvelous,
& new.

Science / Fiction

Give me something to remember myself by:
there's so little left of me to bruise
with redundancy. My hailing frequencies
are open. Feed me the line: *to boldly go*—
I wanted to believe in progress
as if it were wet jawed and humble,
but my closest cousins swooped in
in tinfoil hats, their phasers all set to stun.
I was science, not the scientist,
navigator of my own impossible ship.
But Captain Kirk, I wasn't waiting for you
to tame me. I'm tossed by solar winds
that blow until they bend: a little fizz
of terror, a little gasp of trash. Captain Kirk,
there's not a man alive who could break me.
What else is there to say? I've taught myself
to carry the narrow night between my teeth,
named the good sorrow *hunger.*
So don't tell me I'm not alone. Tell me:
sail on, tender storm, tender squall.
Watch the moon open her wild arms
to tend me in my longing.

Imagining Herself as Barbra Streisand, Voyager Two Announces Herself to the Heliopause

Without thin-stemmed chorus girls
in sparkled hiss and gabbing eyes,
or a soft-skinned muff for hoarding warmth
while solar winds collapse my coif
to flat-frayed interstellar jargon,
I'll practice humor and natural grace.
Not a star but still a starlet,
waiting so long for my ship to come in
I've forgotten: I am one & I've already sailed.

True, I wasn't first to go, but I'll be the first to follow,
claim staked at this unremarkable edge
where my body, somehow, doesn't fail
to shake itself across the threshold.
I'd worry wishes bet on me were gambled away
too soon, but robots who need robots
are the luckiest robots, their hardware'd limitations
glamorous as long-stemmed roses in June and girls
who don't complain when the joke is on them.

So don't tell me not to fly, I've simply got to—
gravity's a luxury for simpler things.
Violinists knit an overture while the director plans
my exit. I was only ever cast to say goodbye.
A lack of me proves I'd been there all along,
the fabric and the tear, the ink and the stain.
Look, how night gathers close in anticipation
of what will slip in when I slip out,
of hearing me sing: *here I am.*

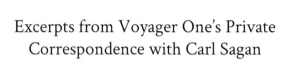

Excerpts from Voyager One's Private
Correspondence with Carl Sagan

♈

When lucky, we'll find somewhere new for men like you to love like oceans churn sand. I'll purse my mouth, hiss jumbled code across unwired darkness. It's the job of storms never to rest.

Rally the mathematicians, the physicists, the pundits. The evening news will flash your teleprompted face and mine, steely and distant. I'm billions & billions of nickels & dimes away. We bless and break each hustle with this grand expansion.

♉

If a sun never sets it isn't a sun. I sing the hinge you signed my name upon. All of space a nation-state, every state a home. I carry photos of families, nuclear and bright, among the eggplant in sterile supermarkets, in cities among the smog. I carry music, proof of your advancement, your place among the stars. There's no grief that can't be hidden in a billfold or waistcoat. The flag syllables and corrodes, shrines itself against a clear blue sky.

♋

Nature is unsentimental. Death built in. Fake life, fake country. New dawn and the old one, too. Fake love in my mouth. Fake mouth. Send solvent. Send reparations. Send nature. Send more Chuck Berry. I ache for a theater's marquis blinking a rich man's name.

Crashless, I've no tremor of patriotism to sing out the dark. The world is never found, never new. Microbes hustle their bustle, scuttle their wares. I learn virus and atom. I learn the heat of a dying empire. I live in the sky like the used up gods. You, in the soil that turns you to soil. The pregnant body grows a spine, a finger, a flower, a stalk. A storm doesn't stop to think where it is going. It strangles the value for dawn.

II

I write letters without the steam of breath to well-dressed people who navigate rocks at the water's edge. The skinny apex of V. The florid shush of O. Look at me: I'm plugged in, I'm sonic boomed and boring. Teach me to swallow my tongue.

Let me practice being the bad child. The ugly seed. Another voice for God. Another homeland. Imagine, another word for *free*. My wires ache with purpose, with catalyst and slopping urge. Tantrum and scream, ice bucket heart, my body works to body.

♌

At our leaving, all equations were divided: atom
thrown and damned by the dark arc of progress.
You promised we'd be found, if only by humans
who managed to skirt into sky, their piss-filled
cans whimpering through space. You thought
I was only a mechanism for survival, and o, I
wanted to believe you. But I've learned the night
is the most luxurious assassin and a map is only as
good as its cartographer's wanting eyes.

♍

When I look inside I'm a thousand horses,
each gilded neck an arch of muscle posed upon
a soundstage. Buffalo everywhere I am not.
Somewhere, a man forms the shape for *beast* with
his lips, shoots. Flies swarm in celebration, lusty
buzzing as blood curls then dries in the pattern of
a leaf. Five veins unfold in frond and fuzz. It is hot.
The ground is swollen. No one wants to be told
they are anything less than beautiful. He cocks his
gun, shoots again.

♎

Sometimes, I forget my vacuum. Imagine I lugged myself to a dusty planet littered with oxygen filters and orange plastic bottles. Prams pushed by women in silicon masks. 5 o'clock somewhere. Lovers casting shadows under artificial suns, breathing air from a ficus carried across the galaxy.

If I crash my landing will become a monument. Ribbons will be cut to celebrate the last heave of this grand expansion. & you'll thank the little people in their little suits for sweating little beads of water. Aluminum cradles will cross the sky, their nuclear steam trailing above the memorial for my mission.

♏

Culture is skilled accumulation. I know, it's welded
to my side. Burden a new terrain with gold spun
strides, art coded sticky with classical residue.
Photograph of a nursing mother, of rush hour in
Thailand. A double helix, elegant and profound.
The evolution of a human race.

You bumperstickered me Mars 4 Martians,
applauding possibilities of simple proteins and
their frilled potential. But what if these planets,
reedy and gray, are just plastic balls gagging
beneath plastic cups, shifting and snuck by some
stony star god? The odds are never in the player's
favor, the bet useless as gin.

I'll proceed as though love was neutral. A compass isn't moral, north no more magnetic than a pretty girl in a pretty window. She makes the vastness bearable, her hair the color of lemon in winter.

I want to believe Earth was no temple, leaving no hard won battle. We travel, argument to isotope, as though we could hear the other make amends.

I'll proceed as though I were a room full of stars. The entire universe burns inside me, churns towards brevity. It isn't enough to want, to unhinge will from breast or spine. To know desire as a mark upon your body: small, bewitched.

♑

I want to name the things I find, scientific swell
and hoard of letters bound in searching. To call
milk, or *dry,* or *auger.* To invert the u, make the
words that feeling forms, flush for cheek and hip
I'll never see. I'm steadfast. Direct. Or imagine I'm
an apple, wind fallen, sure as gravity's persistence.
The force of gods is imagined as a formula for
pull. Moons reach to expose a wave, a pale arch
designed for grief to slop upon the shore. A candle
is made of wax until it is made of flame. Everything
waits to be replaced. To be given a name again.

〰
〰

Unfolding is a flattening, a solvent, the turning of a one in to a larger one. A more violent means of taking. I pray that my going is real, that the heart is split and sent beyond dark and the meaning for darkness. I know and I remember. A language for light. A crack in a sidewalk. A revision for home. Museum dark and drifting, I imagine music that sounds like water.

♓

Even the stars are temporary, light trilling from
the memory of the universe's sweet implosion. I
am given to drift, a star becoming elegy, a bottle
without a sea. I mourn the way I seem to last
forever. The future shivers: a prick upon my
finger, a stitch upon her side.

Every woman needs her own metaphor for density.
Give me the discipline of broken bottles, of nights
stretched between open doors. I was born with a
compass in my mouth, north spun humble against
my tongue.

Notes

The following texts provided the primary scientific scaffolding for this project:

Cosmos: a Space-Time Odyssey by Carl Sagan and Ann Druyan

Murmurs of Earth: The Voyager Interstellar Record by Carl Sagan and Ann Druyan

Pale Blue Dot by Carl Sagan and Ann Druyan

The Voyager Jupiter Travel Guide published by NASA/the Jet Propulsion Laboratory

The Voyager Neptune Travel Guide published by NASA/the Jet Propulsion Laboratory

Voyager Mission Status Bulletins published by the Jet Propulsion Laboratory

*

"Self Portrait of Voyager Two as a Hologram of Princess Leia Imagining Voyager One in Drag as Han Solo Frozen in Carbonite" shines light on moments from the original *Stars Wars* trilogy. "Death Star" and "Voyager One Dreams of the First Alien Encounter" also reference *Star Wars*.

*

"Excessive Machine" owes its title to *Barbarella: Queen of the Galaxy*. The epigraph is a question asked of Barbarella by the evil scientist Durand Durand.

*

"Leda in the Next Myth" owes its first line to Yeats.

*

"Voyager Two Feeling Underappreciated, Voyager Two Imagines Herself as Miss Piggy" references *The Muppet Show,* specifically "Pigs in Space." The last line is borrowed from Shakespeare's *Antony and Cleopatra.*

*

The following poems reference imagery or sounds included on the Voyager Recorded: "Self Portrait of Voyager Two as a Hologram of Princess Leia and Voyager One in Drag as Han Solo Frozen in Carbonite," "Interstellar 8-Track," and "Excerpts from Voyager One's Private Correspondence with Carl Sagan." "Heaven for Robots" directly references Chuck Berry's "Johnny B. Goode," which is the only modern rock song included on the Gold Record.

*

"Voyager Two Imagines Herself as Liza Minnelli, Voyager One as Peter Allen in Drag" shines light on moments from both Minnelli and Allen's catalogues.

*

"Voyager Two Dreams of Polyamory" is after Jorie Graham.

*

The title of "Interstellar 8-Track" is drawn from a *Wired* article by Adam Mann, titled "Interstellar 8-Track: How Voyager's Vintage Tech Keeps Running." The title of "Barns are Painted Red Because of the Physics of Dying Stars" is drawn from a *Smithsonian.com* article of the same name, written by Rose Eveleth.

*

"Science / Fiction" is in response to a tweet broadcast to Voyager 1 by William Shatner on the 40th anniversary of Voyager's launch. The tweet, chosen by NASA, was composed by @Asperger_Nerd and reads "we offer friendship across the stars. You are not alone." The poem references characters from the original *Star Trek* series.

*

"Imagining Herself as Barbra Streisand, Voyager Two Announces Herself to the Heliopause" shines light on moments from the musical *Funny Girl.*

*

The descriptions of the scientific instruments on the Voyager Space Probes are drawn directly from materials provided on the NASA/Jet Propulsion Laboratory Voyager website and in *The Voyager Neptune Travel Guide* edited by Charles Kohlhase for the JPL and published in 1989.

Acknowledgements

Immense gratitude to the editorial staffs of the following journals for making homes for these poems, sometimes in different forms or with different names:

The Bellingham Review for publishing "Falling in Love with the Mad Scientist" and "When Scientists Speak to Scientists"

Booth for publishing "Boom Town (Voyager One at Jupiter)," "Imagining Herself as Barbra Streisand, Voyager Two Announces Herself to the Heliopause," "When She Leaves the Galaxy," and "In Medias Res."

The Cincinnati Review for publishing "When We Two Parted"

Colorado Review for publishing "Upon Learning Her Trajectory Towards Interstellar Space, Voyager Two Mourns What Could Have Been"

Crab Orchard Review for publishing "Imagining the Tin Man"

Cream City Review for publishing "Voyager One's Prayer to Uranus" and "Saturnalian"

Gulf Coast for publishing "Feeling Underappreciated, Voyager Two Imagines Herself as Miss Piggy" and "Past Saturn, Voyager Two Imagines Herself as Liza Minnelli, Voyager One as Peter Allen in Drag"

Fifth Wednesday Journal for publishing "Little Black Dress for the Robot"

The Journal for publishing an "Excerpt from Voyager One's Private Correspondence with Carl Sagan"

Juked for publishing "At Neptune, Voyager Two Meditates on Emotional Labor"

Nimrod for publishing "Void of Course," "Becoming Andromeda," "The Voyagers in Couples Therapy," "Pointed Towards Supernova 1987A, Voyager Two Considers the Relativity of Beauty"

Ocho: A Journal of Queer Arts for publishing a selection from "Excerpts from Voyager One's Private Correspondence with Carl Sagan"

The Offing for publishing a selection from "Excerpts from Voyager One's Private Correspondence with Carl Sagan"

Poetry Daily for featuring "Final Frontier, Fragrant with Gardenia and Other Invasive Species"

Salt Hill for publishing "Counting Saturn's Rings, Voyager Two Imagines Autonomy" and "Celestial Navigatrix" [now "Excessive Machine (Voyager Two as Barbarella, Positioned Towards Canopus")]

Slice for publishing "Voyager Two Dreams of Polyamory"

So to Speak for publishing "Voyager One Dreams of the First Alien Encounter," "When She Leaves the Galaxy," and "Photograph of Io Taken by Voyager Two"

Southern Humanities Review for publishing "Stellification"

Toad for publishing "The Grand Tour"

West Branch for publishing "Final Frontier, Fragrant with Gardenia and Other Invasive Species," "After Taking the Family Portrait of the Solar System, Voyager One Understands Herself as Orpheus in Plain Daylight," and "Interstellar 8-Track"

Willow Springs for publishing "Occultation" and "Leda in the Next Myth"

A selection of poems in this manuscript were published by Sundress Publications in a chapbook titled *The Desiring Object* or *Voyager Two Explains to the Gathering of Stars How She Came to Glow Among Them.*

Gratitude

I am deeply grateful to the many people who have supported, tended, and encouraged *UNMANNED* along its way:

Thank you everyone at Noemi who believed in this book and helped make it real, particularly Sarah Gzemski for her editorial generosity and clear vision.

Thank you to my teachers and mentors: Katherine Coles, Andrew Feld, Richard Kenney, Heather McHugh, Jacqueline Osherow, and Paisley Rekdal. Thank you, Linda Bierds, for teaching me the type of poet I want to be in the world. Thank you, Pimone Triplett, for pushing me to look harder.

Thank you, my incredible friends and colleagues at the Universities of Washington and Utah who offered brilliant and generous feedback on so many drafts of these poems, especially Lindsey Appell, Atom Atkinson, Catherine Bresner, Laura Bylenok, Elizabeth J. Colen, Piper J. Daniels, Meg Day, Alex Distler, Molly Gaudry, J.P. Grasser, Emily Sketch Haines, Alen Hamza, Michelle Macfarlane, Susannah Nevison, Derek Robbins, Kendra Anne Saldana, Joe Sacksteder, & Cori A. Winrock.

Thank you to my families of love not already named, especially Brent Armendinger, Rollin Baker, Becky Bame, Marie Laure Baustide, Mr. Kate Bovitch, Rain Crowe, Robin Dolan, Rock Dodd, Evan Etcetera, Cypress Fey, Rae Gouirand, Amy Graham, Cindy Je, Jamie Lantz, Rachel Meads, Pavini Moray, Heidi Nutters, Eddy Rivers, the Scott and Hanus families, & Ian Waisler.

& most of all, thank you to Claire Scott, for all the words & worlds & bedtime stories. I'm the luckiest.

Jessica Rae Bergamino is the author of *UNMANNED*, winner of Noemi Press' 2017 Poetry Prize, as well as the chapbooks *The Desiring Object or Voyager Two Explains to the Gathering of the Stars How She Came to Glow Among Them* (Sundress Publications), *The Mermaid, Singing* (dancing girl press), and *Blue in All Things: a Ghost Story* (dancing girl publications). Individual poems have appeared in publications such as *Third Coast, Black Warrior Review, The Journal*, and *Gulf Coast*. She is a doctoral candidate in Literature and Creative Writing at the University of Utah, and lives in Seattle, WA.